W9-BWG-430

THE ART OF

SUN TZU

~~~~~~~

A New Translation by

MICHAEL NYLAN

THE
ART
OF
WAR

W. W. NORTON & COMPANY

Independent Publishers Since 1923

For information about permission to reproduce selections from this
book, write to Permissions, W. W. Norton & Company, Inc.,
500 Fifth Avenue, New York, NY 10110

For information about special discounts for bulk purchases, please contact
W. W. Norton Special Sales at specialsales@wwnorton.com or 800-233-4830

Manufacturing by Lake Book Manufacturing
Book design by Lovedog Studio
Production manager: Julia Druskin

Library of Congress Cataloging-in-Publication Data

Names: Sunzi, active 6th century B.C., author. | Nylan, Michael, translator.
Title: The art of war / Sun Tzu ; a new translation by Michael Nylan.
Other titles: Sunzi bing fa. English
Description: First edition. | New York : W. W. Norton & Company,
2020. | Includes bibliographical references.
Identifiers: LCCN 2019027150 | ISBN 9781324004899 (hardcover) |
ISBN 9781324004905 (epub)
Subjects: LCSH: Military art and science—Early works to 1800.
Classification: LCC U101 .S93213 2020 | DDC 355.02—dc23
LC record available at https://lccn.loc.gov/2019027150

W. W. Norton & Company, Inc., 500 Fifth Avenue, New York, N.Y. 10110
www.wwnorton.com

W. W. Norton & Company Ltd., 15 Carlisle Street, London W1D 3BS

1 2 3 4 5 6 7 8 9 0

Contents

INTRODUCTION

ANYONE TAKING UP A BOOK like *The Art of War* (*Sunzi,* or, in one romanization, *Sun Tzu*) wonders who wrote it, what is it good for, and how do we understand it now, so many centuries after it was compiled?[1] This brief introduction to the Norton translation tries to answer those basic questions in four short sections, probing the problem of *The Art of War*'s ultimate message to readers today.

WHO WROTE *THE ART OF WAR*?

By the experts' current understanding, all early Chinese texts are "composite texts," texts compiled over time from impressive rhetoric ascribed to certain authors, often on vague impressions and little or no evidence. *The Art of War* (*Sunzi bingfa* 孫子兵法) is no exception to this general rule.

Compiled in the last century or so of the Zhan-guo period (475–221 BCE),[2] the work doubtless represents insights garnered over long centuries by different hands, possibly even by experts operating in different locations. That said, up to today, later writers, whether commentators or not, have generally accepted the same long-standing tradition: that *The Art of War* text was compiled by Sunzi (Sun Wu 孫武, or Sun Tzu), who served the king of Wu 吳 in the late sixth century BCE. However gratifying this tale, it cannot be verified at this remove, and indeed is unlikely to be true.

Although a Sunzi (Master Sun) makes a brief appearance in the *Lüshi chunqiu* 呂氏春秋 (compiled ca. 238 BCE), Sun Wu, the legendary general to whom *The Art of War* is ascribed, does not appear "on record" before Sima Qian's *Historical Records* or *Shiji* (compiled ca. 90 BCE) composes a biography for him. (An excavated manuscript from around the same time as the *Shiji* bears witness to Sun Wu's immense fame as military master, however.) Before the second century of Western Han rule, then, the Sun Wu legend is nearly complete: this Sunzi is the advisor who persuaded King Helu of Wu to adopt a new mode of warfare, deploying mass infantry troops rather than nobles in four-horse chariots—a method credited with gaining Helu's stunning victory over his neighbor, mighty Chu, in 506 BCE. Sunzi's method and tactics are summarized in Sima Qian's biography in one memorable scene where Sunzi drills 180 of the king's concubines in the new tight battle formations he envisions, and dares to behead two of them who disobey his orders. Having persuaded the palace women that they should follow him "through heaven and earth," he goes on to lead the men of Wu by similar methods to an easy defeat of Wu's rival.

The problem is this: that Sun Wu alone, in stark contrast to such heroes as Wu Zixu and Pang Juan, does not figure in any of the early masterworks that lovingly detail the complex maneuvers of the southern kingdom of Wu. For this reason, scholars since the twelfth century have repeatedly queried the historicity of the Sunzi narrative. The doubters have explored a range of explanations for the anomaly: (1) that Sun Wu never existed, and he is no more than a doppelgänger for Wu Zixu; (2) that Sun Bin, a better-attested general working 150 years later for Qi, needed a respectable forebear, and so a Sun Wu ("Sun the Martial") was devised to fill that role by a person or persons unknown; (3)

that Sun Wu, whether he existed or not, is credited with the same characteristics as all other military geniuses in the story cycles; and (4) that listeners and readers well versed in the rhetoric of high cultural learning within manuscript culture freely invented and adapted usable pasts to any pressing matters at hand.

There is an old joke among classicists: "The *Iliad* was not written by Homer, but by somebody else with the same name." This saying could be easily adapted to apply to *The Art of War* ascribed to Sunzi, as moderns today have no access to more biographical material about this master than we find in passages of fairly late date. Unless one can prove that the Sunzi who wrote *The Art of War* is the same general Sunzi who drilled the king's concubines and won the Battle of Boju, then the text might as well be compiled "by somebody else with the same name." That said, the Western Han stories about Sunzi reveal the presumption that people at the court of the time entertained about the residents of the far-distant southeastern coast of China: that they were prepared to use any ruthless methods when fighting, since they had little awareness or appreciation of the elaborate ritual code that in theory restricted the honorable courses of action open to the high-ranking officers on the North China plain. Yet these same officers' frequent resort to expedient alliances in the centuries leading up to unification by Qin in 221 BCE, coupled with their frank admiration for the professionalism shown by the "dare to die" soldiers drawn from the ranks of the commoners, soon challenged and complicated earlier notions of aristocratic honor throughout the territory we call "China" today.

Whereas a late fifth-century BCE army rarely fielded more than 50,000 troops, by 260 BCE the kingdom of Zhao fielded an army of 400,000 to resist a Qin invasion, and by 225 BCE General Wang Jian 王翦 (fl. 230–ca. 210) of Qin requested a force of 600,000 men for his invasion of Chu. The early histories may well exaggerate the sizes of these armies. Nonetheless, such descriptions convey a sense of the power of the centralizing states to levy enormous infantry armies at short notice and supply these armies on protracted campaigns far from home. Annexations of the weaker states brought newly conquered men and materiel, further enhancing the conqueror's ability to build roads, man forts, call up military recruits, and increase taxes, which, in turn, grew the war machine to conquer more territory. Thus peasant soldiers became key to the ruler's power in the early empires of late Zhanguo, Qin, and Western Han.

That policy makers generally regarded them as such helps to explain the surprising thrust of many masterworks from the early empires—not just "Confucian" texts—urging upon the rulers of the day a "politics of the common good." Their reasoning was this: if the lowly commoner is to give his total allegiance to the ruler's war efforts, he merits a certain measure of consideration from his liege. The ruler should look to feeding and housing him and listening to his complaints, for it was such people who prop up the ship of state like deep waters. In addition, peasant soldiers must be credited with immortal souls, if they are to entertain any hopes of adequate requital for their sacrifices on behalf of the ruling house. Hints of this willingness to rethink the bases for honor and patriotism emerge in some *Art of War* passages, even as others treat the infantry like animals to be herded toward their deaths. But that is a major story that lies in the main beyond first readings of *The Art of War*.

WHAT IS THE WORK ASCRIBED
TO SUNZI GOOD FOR?

Like the general public, military men and textual scholars have long debated whether the ultimate message of *The Art of War* text is pro-war or anti-war. By some accounts, Ho Chi Minh, his General Giap, and Mao Zedong scoured the text in order to plot their next strategic moves (although not a few dispute these claims). At the same time, the text urges upon its followers the notion that it is better to outthink the enemy than to fight him, in part because of the devastating costs of war. Any fair reading of the text ultimately depends on how much weight the reader puts on the introductory versus the concluding chapters of *The Art of War.* Chapter 13 of *The Art of War* calculates coolly, for instance: "As a rule of thumb, to raise 100,000 troops and send them out on campaign to a location 1,000 leagues away costs 1,000 units of gold/ day, including the expenses incurred by the Hundred Families and the upkeep by the ruling house."[3] The last chapters of the *The Art of War* are full of this sort of dovish rhetoric. Far from delivering a rousing call to arms for casual warmongering, *The Art of War* continually asks, explicitly and implicitly, whether other means, ranging from diplomacy to deceit, cannot be better deployed in service to the nation. Admittedly, this is a message that many readers down through the ages have preferred to ignore, since *The Art of War* meanwhile teaches field commanders how to secure final victory, if possible, and honorable retreat, when necessary.

What is not up for debate, then, is the emphasis that *The Art of War* places on strategic thinking. Nor can its massive influence be denied—in both the expected contexts (military planning and battlefield engagements) and in the unexpected (sex manuals, contemporary business guides, bureaucratic manuals, and so on). As strategic thinking proves essential in so many professions and walks of life, *The Art of War* has gained adherents in improbable quarters, not just at West Point and Harvard Business School. A small selection of those "alternative" readings is therefore cited here, for the reader's delectation:

1. in games of skill (e.g., archery contests, games of chess), where celebrity is gained by those who can deliver reliable victories;

2. in academic careers, since warfare is a surprisingly common metaphor in the history

of scholarship, and very popular in the early empires in China;[4]

3. in business ventures (Bai Gui, whose mercantile acumen prompted the Wei kingdom's ruler to recruit him for high office, ran his business "as a general would," we are told);

4. in sexual dalliances, with their lively "thrust and parry";

5. in medical practices, where an illness, portrayed as an invasion, must be overcome.

Doubtless, students of Sino-American relations will find intriguing the tale of *The Art of War*'s introduction to American readers via a careful translation by Brigadier General Samuel B. Griffith II (d. 1983) during the American Vietnam War (1954–1975). Griffith's translation of *The Art of War* played a vital role in spurring revisionist treatments of the Chinese Communists during the 1960s and 1970s, wherein Mao's faithful figured as anything but Soviet automatons. Tracing the ups and downs of *The Art of War*'s legacy in the United States can open a window onto the assumptions that the U.S. military has brought to Cold War, post–Cold War, and Trump-era policies, even as

The Art of War participates in a much broader spectrum of the American imagination.

Even before becoming president, Donald Trump tweeted Sunzi wisdom to his followers.[5] Trump, unlikely to have read *The Art of War*, included its enthusiasts in his administration. Steve Bannon was a missionary for Sunzi.[6] Sebastian Gorka, former deputy assistant to the president, sported a vanity license plate: "Art War."[7] Neither Bannon nor Gorka lasted long in the White House, but they were hardly alone in their fondness for the military classic. Ex-Secretary of Defense James Mattis, a retired Marine Corps general, remains true to General Griffith's tradition. Mattis commented about his reading on strategy:

> You've got to know Sun-tzu and Carl von Clausewitz, of course. The Army was always big on Clausewitz, the Prussian; the Navy on Alfred Thayer Mahan, the American; and the Air Force on Giulio Douhet, the Italian. But the Marine Corps has always been more Eastern-oriented. I am much more comfortable with Sun-tzu and his approach to warfare.[8]

Hmm. The question is, Did Mattis deploy *The Art of War* while maneuvering in the White House? Apparently, not much. Perhaps there are just too many cryptic lines in the *The Art of War* ascribed to Sunzi.

WHY READ THIS CLASSIC TODAY?

Why read *The Art of War* today? One may as well ask, why read anything today? If pressed to extract a single overriding "message" from the text, it would be this: *Perform your calculations for everything liable to calculation, but also think very deeply about what people are capable of.* The book opens with talk about how to unify the wills of elites and those without access to great power,[9] and it alludes to the vagaries of people in all ranks and walks of life, only to end with an inquiry into success and failure that lays great stress on the concrete intelligence provided by defectors and spies. This makes for riveting reading, especially in an age when big data and artificial intelligence *seem* to suggest that human beings as a species are more malleable than we'd like to think, while the Internet purveys an often hostile world, replete with a host of new bat-tlefields.[10] One fine observation supplied by *The Art of War* makes sense: closer acquaintance with the past—and especially the stories told about compelling figures in the past, whether good or bad, wise or too smart for their own good—helps to prepare the thinking person to become a better judge of options in the current sociopolitical realm.[11] There is no good reason to believe that the past was any simpler than the present.[12] And this form of fore-thought is all the more incumbent, given the complex challenges now confronting global citizens, since the direst calamities can ensue from failures to generate more nuanced assessments that factor in the long-term and inadvertent consequences of apparently attractive proposals. The Iraq invasion or the Brexit mess, to take two recent examples, clearly reflect refusals to engage in long-range plan-ning and to probe common stereotypes.

That may explain why Sunzi's *The Art of War* turns up more and more frequently in daily life in these United States. When Speaker of the House Nancy Pelosi stared down Donald Trump over his demand for billions for a border wall, her col-league James Clyburn of South Carolina intro-duced her to fellow lawmakers as the Sunzi of her day, only slightly mangling his citation of the Chinese classic in the process.[13] Doubtless, *The Art of War* has assumed such an exalted place in the western world because "war is the force that gives our lives meaning," and "we all, alas, live in a war zone now."[14] Then, too, we are so apt to define power by violent action, drinking deep from the metaphors for life that highlight struggle, that it seems only natural to us that lessons from war will help us in the office or on the sports field. And our certainty of this is heightened when we turn to games, to computer programs like AlphaZero, or to mathematical algorithms to decide the "right" solution for competing schemes.

Even to those who have acquired good judgment, a major problem persists, however, insofar as operations in real life in real time always are based on imperfect information, and that means we must be very nimble at responding to surprises and excesses, since human foibles ultimately determine the outcome of so many events. As the eleventh-century polymath Su Shi observed, "If the heavens conformed so perfectly to a measure, then even an untutored . . . child could calculate its movements over a thousand years with ease. But due to inconsistences and what doesn't fit the measurements, even the most clever reckoner cannot fully grasp its operations."[15] The human heart is equally mysterious. The good commander, for this reason, must have *real* intelligence (in both senses of that word). He must know the basics of human psychology (the uses of fear, the advantages of carrots versus sticks, etc.), but he must also have a strong sense of the unimaginable richness and variety of human experience. Pavlovian rewards do not motivate people nearly as well as social scientists once assumed.[16]

To that end, reading *The Art of War* schools us in the significance of three Chinese concepts that barely figure in the comparable Western discussions, but are nonetheless crucial when we contemplate any arena of rule-free action:

> quan 權 ("contingency"; "balance of forces";
>   the careful weighing of options);
> shi 勢 ("disposition" or "strategic position"),
>   and
> shi 時 ("timing" and "timely opportunity").

Whenever we innovate, or whenever irregular, unpredictable, or unprecedented situations arise, as they do so often in modern life, we take the plunge, whether we welcome it or not, trying to find our way to a constructive outcome. Prudence demands that due heed to fixed rules be tempered by more flexible approaches, if the long-term well-being of the physical body, the social circle, and the body politic is to be achieved or maintained. As every beginning student of Chinese culture soon learns, thinkers in early China did not admire rule-based behavior as extravagantly as do ethicists in the modern West, schooled in the Kantian or neo-Kantian moral ("categorical") imperatives. So *The Art of War*, no less than the *Analects* ascribed to Confucius or Laozi's *Tao Te Ching*, trains the thinking person in the subtle art of knowing when to stick to the rules and when to toss them aside. "Stubbornness in sticking to a plan" likely spells doom to the unwary, as Chapter 3 warns.

It matters, too, that *The Art of War* brings us around to the commonsensical "politics of the common good," a line of reasoning seeking mutual benefit that deserves far greater attention today, as a valuable corrective to the Gordon Gekkos of the corporate and political world, with their cynical views on what matters in human life. Let us begin with the fact that the initial preparations for war were made in the temple, in the presence of the ancestors, because guidance of every sort was

sought in fraught undertakings, even when the violence was sanctioned.[17] Moreover, *The Art of War*
ends with a quiet coda whose firm assertion is too
often overlooked: that even the most impressive
empires fall as soon as their rulers, by their care-
less conduct, lose or cast aside the best men in their
employ. So while duplicity and deception have
their places in war, the one constant central to both
victory in wars and stable order in peacetime is the
good will and mutual trust that binds ruler, commander, and their men together.

Granted, readers who are so inclined can easily
find ways to read into the more enigmatic lines of
The Art of War advice to manipulate anyone who
is vulnerable, but such readings would not sit well
with the most admired masterworks devoted to
ethical, legal, political, and religious issues in the
early empires in China. These classics insist that
those in power may not hold cheap the predilec-
tions and desires of their subordinates. As Chapter
10 says, the best commander is he whose "sole concern is to protect his men and promote his ruler's
interests," with those interests defined in the final
Chapter 13 in terms of humanity and humaneness. Accordingly, the able commander gauges the
morale of his men constantly, anxious to do right

by them since all are joined in a single endeavor wherein the loss of one is a loss to all.[18] Needless to say, the commander sometimes has no alternative but to sacrifice some of his men, in the hope of preserving countless others who would otherwise be killed, enslaved, or raped, but he is acutely aware of the gravity of his decisions. Concepts developed in *The Art of War* may foster in today's readers the will to formulate more realistic guidelines for taking action or retreating, without blindsiding either the person or valued allies. The goal is to deflect attacks from others, whenever humanly possible.[19]

Perhaps the most profound message derived from *The Art of War* (one of immense relevance today) is that any victory depends upon knowing oneself at least as well as the other party cast as the obstruction. Know thyself, *The Art of War* enjoins the reader, before trying to command others in matters great and small.[20] "Collapse comes when ... a senior officer ... fails to understand [his own capacities]."[21] For character counts and character tells, sooner or later—all the more so in tricky situations. Those in charge must exemplify "wisdom, reliability, humaneness, courage, and strictness,"[22] Sunzi tells us, lest widespread disaffection thin the ranks and bring disasters in its wake. The wise leader in *The Art of War* has infinite patience for correcting his or her own flaws, if only because the leader creates the conditions for internal and external strength, "but whether the enemy can be conquered or not rests with him."[23] Courage thus entails a clear-eyed willingness to reckon what likely can and cannot be changed, opening a path not too dissimilar from Dorothy Day's "The life you save may be your own." It involves knowing when to expend scarce resources to attain a greater good. For that reason, the ideal commander does not let himself be "encumbered" by the dismal thought of the individual lives that face ruin, lest his mixed emotions impede the methodical planning and execution of the war that is his primary responsibility.[24]

True leadership is not craven, in the sense that it does not feed upon celebrity, as "the finest way to win a battle" is not necessarily one that "the whole realm applauds."[25] Often victories on behalf of others take years to realize; only the very unwise expect or need instant gratifications. While it takes little to see this in the abstract, we have to have such lessons repeatedly affirmed before we know them in our guts, and *The Art of War* continually prompts readers to push such basic insights further. For *The Art of*

War teaches that the truly able person, by definition, is a reliably good judge when confronting tense situations: the "hard work pays off in reliable ways."[26]

Meanwhile, *The Art of War* conveys astute observations about the psychological compulsions that cause people to behave in inexplicable ways in certain circumstances, especially under stress. In one surprising example of this, Master Sun recommends that generals deliberately position their men in seemingly hopeless situations, knowing that anything less than a desperate army cannot possibly win against the odds: "Only if you plunge them into places with no way out will you and your men stay alive."[27] It is no shame, then, in *The Art of War* for officers and grunts to share their fears of death or acknowledge the fellow humanity of their opponents, even though the heat of battle requires eagerness to launch sudden strikes.[28]

The Art of War is a classic, and by consensus in early China a "classic" is a work that says neither too little nor too much. It provokes thought and reflection because of what it does not say, as much as what it baldly states. Moreover, a "classic" has wide applicability to a range of human dilemmas. Granted, many moderns will prefer to read passages from *The Art of War* out of context, pigeonholing it as a "military classic" or a cool guidebook to strategic gamesmanship of little relevance outside the battlefield. *The Art of War* is much, much more than that, as becomes evident once a little effort is made to bridge the distance between today's world and that of the original readers two millennia ago.

Any classic work generates multiple readings:

1. the meaning it had for its author or compiler, within the textual community that generated it and to which it was addressed;
2. the meaning or meanings it acquired over time, down through tradition(s) (usually plural);
3. the meaning it holds for people today (often quite different from meanings 1 and 2).

Does it matter, then, that with *The Art of War* we cannot retrieve meaning #1 at all, not knowing its author or date of compilation, or that we find it difficult to keep track of the multiple meanings it acquired over time? Probably not as much as pedants think. Still, careful readers might bear in mind the following two points:

First, if we attend to the realities of the past, a

key figure invoked in the narratives from the early empires is the free landowning farmer who also served in the army and routinely fought for hearth and home—a figure who may seem, at first glance, to be an early equivalent of the modern soldier in the national army. Still, the pitched struggles in the premodern period were as much about family honor as about individual glory, while the actual struggles of heroes (military and nonmilitary) tended to be more personal (spurred, for example, by the desire for a name for personal bravery and martial virtue or for revenge)—and not only because there were no drones to reduce casualties to "collateral damage." Simply put, the spillage of blood and guts was not then dedicated to the all-devouring abstraction that is the nation-state, a larger collective or imagined community bound by little but impersonal trust.[29] Readers should note the preoccupation with the "commander" in every chapter of this translation, to whom all soldiers owe their loyalty, especially if he commits himself to the commoner-soldier's welfare.

Second, what further impedes more informed readings of the *The Art of War* is the common (mis) perception that the Chinese always preferred promotion of the civil arts over the martial. Several essays in the forthcoming Norton Critical Edition of *The Art of War* take up this topic, demonstrating that it is essentially a modern argument imposed on the distant past in China. Huan Tan, for example, one of the most famous Confucian masters of the first century BCE, studied the Five Classics with a court classicist and swordsmanship with a sword-master. In mid-Ming, Wang Yangming (1472–1529) won renown as both an idealist thinker and a canny general. *The Art of War* has become a classic precisely because it is *not* merely a technical manual registering a sharp distinction between military and civil life, a dichotomy too obvious for the most sophisticated masters in antiquity to dwell upon.

Bringing a bit of historical depth to *The Art of War* means the astute reader can travel beyond principles of strategy to investigate the very cultural bedrock of contemporary China, while circumventing the shifting sands of cultural essentialism. Such readers will want to consider how strongly *The Art of War* speaks to multiple situations, also the text's insistence that we forge connections between our own goals and the lives of those we interact with and materially affect.

WHY READ THIS NORTON TRANSLATION IN PARTICULAR?

Okay, you have decided to read *The Art of War,* but why read this particular translation, when so many are available, including one with a foreword written by General David Petraeus, telling us that "Sunzi's classic work is, in short, . . . every bit as relevant now as when it was written"? After all, the language of *The Art of War* is deceptively simple, a delicious aspect of a work which treats deception and self-deception with utter seriousness. Throughout, *The Art of War* uses familiar, almost rudimentary vocabulary, but redefines the graphs in subtle ways. The primary meaning of *quan* 權 in modern Chinese, for instance, is "power," and yet *The Art of War* never employs the graph in this way. The more familiar the vocabulary, the greater the potential pitfalls for the translator mindful that every word counts and every reading must strive to throw off as much light as the original text. Responsible translation entails far more than cycling through the available translations for many basic terms, in consequence. Visualizing the situations that Sunzi describes, seeing the landscapes and locations that he sketches, then devising alternate scenarios (and hence alternate translations) for nearly every line—this is demanding but necessary work.

Compare a brief passage from Chapter 5 in several well-known translations:

Lionel Giles (1910):

"Simulated disorder postulates perfect discipline; simulated fear postulates courage; simulated weakness postulates strength. Hiding order beneath the cloak of disorder is simply a question of subdivision; concealing courage under a show of timidity presupposes a fund of latent energy; masking strength with weakness is to be effected by tactical dispositions."

Samuel P. Griffith (1963):

"Apparent confusion is a product of good order; apparent cowardice, of courage; apparent weakness, of strength. Order or disorder depends on organization; courage or cowardice on circumstances; strength or weakness on dispositions."

Roger Ames (1993):

"Disorder is born from order; cowardice from courage; weakness from strength. The line between disorder and order lies in logistics; between cowardice and courage, in strategic advantage; and between weakness and strength, in strategic positioning."

Michael Nylan (2020):
"Disorder is born from order; cowardice, from courage; weakness, from strength. Wresting order from disorder depends upon a proper division of the army units; wresting courage from cowardice depends upon assuming a strategic position; wresting strength from weakness depends upon making a certain show."

As is evident, each translation imagines a plausible scenario, but the roles of deception and disposition contrast starkly.

For three years, an international group of scholars drawn from multiple disciplines has pored over successive drafts of this translation, with the intention of making *The Art of War* speak more powerfully to general readers and specialists alike, East and West.[30] Members of the working group included a former military officer and a poet, as well as the usual sampling of academics. This particular array of expertise has been critical to the Norton translation of *The Art of War.* Invariably we began work on a particular chapter by congratulating ourselves that *this* chapter, at least, was "pretty straightforward." Before the hour was out, we'd be stuck in the mire, hacking our way through clusters of synonyms and parsing the fine implications of "terrain," "territory," and "lands," or "state," "kingdom," and "realm." No word escaped the group's notice, and that is as it should be.

Here is where I thank my lucky stars that so many talents were willing to work with me on this translation. No matter how skilled the individual translator, there are limits to one person's imagination, one person's reading, and one person's knowledge. I believe that this edition of *The Art of War* provides the richest possible readings for a spare and allusive text that repays sustained analysis, compels our respect, and still raises big questions after two thousand years of close reading.

A Note on the Text

The text translated for Norton comes from a standard edition, *Sunzi shijia jizhu* 孫子十家集注 (Collected Commentaries by Ten Masters for the *Sunzi*), with thirteen chapters, first published by Ji Tianbao 吉天保 (late Northern Song),[1] and reprinted by Shanghai guji chubanshe, in 1922, and, more recently, by Shulin. This translation places the greatest weight on the early commentaries to the evolving *Sunzi* tradition, particularly that by Cao Cao 曹操 (155–220 CE). Occasional reference has meanwhile been made to the counterpart to the *Sunzi* found in the Yinqueshan tomb (sealed before 118 BCE?).[2]

THE ART OF WAR

CHAPTER 1

FIRST
CALCULATIONS

始計

ARMS ARE A VITAL MATTER FOR THE ruling house, says Master Sun.[1] As the arena of life and death, as the path to survival or ruin, this subject merits due reflection. Hence the five considerations that must always be kept before you when gauging the strength of the two sides and investigating the true conditions, so as to arrive at a good grasp of the situation: (1) the Way; (2) the heavens; (3) the earth; (4) the field commander; and (5) the regulations.

The "Way," by definition, refers to whatever allows the people and their superior to be of one will, and therefore willing to live or die with him, undeterred by danger. The heavens refers to night and day, heat and frost, in the seasonal rounds. The earth refers to the relative distances, the gradient and openness of the terrain, insofar as this makes

for life or death. Field commanders are defined
by wisdom, reliability, humaneness, courage, and
strictness. Regulations refers to organization and
management, the delegation of authority, and the
deployment of resources. Every field commander
has heard of these Five Constants, but only those
who truly understand them grasp victory.

So, to "gauge the two sides and investigate the true
conditions," I say, I know who will win or lose,
depending on

> which ruler has the Way,
> which commander is the abler,*†
> whose side earth and heaven favor,
> whose rules and orders are obeyed,*
> whose troops are the stronger,*
> whose soldiers, better trained,
> whose rewards and sanctions are more clearly
>   ordained.*

If you employ the commanders who heed my
advice you will win, so retain them. Commanders

† Asterisks in the text indicate rhyme in the original.

who do not will be defeated, however, so dismiss
them.[2] If you've calculated the advantages, and
so have come to see the wisdom of heeding my
advice, then create a favorable strategic disposition,[3] which will, in turn, assist you with matters
beyond it.[4] "Strategic disposition" means wresting
advantages from the conditions at hand and con-
trolling contingencies.

Warfare is the art of deception.
So when you can, feign incapacity,
And when deploying troops, appear to have no
    such plans.
When close, seem to them to be far away, and
    when far away, seem near.
If the enemy commander is avid for advantage, use
    it to lure him in;
If he is volatile, seize upon that;
If he is solid, prepare well for battle;
If he is strong, evade him.
If he is angry, rile him.
If he is unpresuming, feed his arrogance.
If he is rested, tire him out.
If his troops are like family, drive a wedge
    between them.

Attack him when he's unprepared; appear suddenly when he least expects it.

In these lie the expert's victory in arms. Such strategies are not to be divulged beforehand, nor can
they be taught before the battle.[5] Now, the one
who has the most tallies in the "temple calculations" before battle will surely be victorious over
the one with fewer, let alone the one who has no
tallies at all![6] From this I conclude that victory
and defeat can be foreseen.

CHAPTER 2

INITIATING BATTLE

作戰

MASTER SUN SAYS,
In the main, the rules for deploying troops require
these:

    a thousand four-horse light chariots;
    a thousand leather-clad carts;
    ten thousand armored soldiers;
    enough provisions for a thousand leagues.

As a rule, attend to

    the foreign and domestic outlays;
    the expenditures for clients and retainers;
    the resources needed to buy glues and lacquers;[1]
    the initial price and upkeep of chariots and
        armor; plus
    a thousand ingots of gold for daily expenses in
        the field.

Only when these are taken care of will it be feasible to raise 100,000 troops. Once you've committed to a campaign,[2] you should know that, if the victory is long in coming, both your soldiers and their weapons will lose their edge. Should you lay siege to a walled city, you may cripple your troop strength. And if your legions are exposed to the elements for too long, the court's outlays will never suffice.[3] Now, as we all know, the local lords will be quick to pounce on any weaknesses, such as when your soldiers and your weapons are less sharp, and you wil have squandered both your troop strength and your stores. No matter how many clever advisors are at your beck and call, they will never find a way to secure a good outcome. This explains why we have all heard of victories that result from a quick strike by a mediocre opponent, but we have yet to hear of a single victory gained by clever schemers who let the hostilities drag on. In short, there has never been a single instance where the court has profited from lengthy engagements. Therefore, if those in power are not fully aware of the harm that may come from using troops, then they can never truly understand the advantages to be gained from deploying troops.

An expert good at deployment never needs a

second troop call-up or a third round of requisitioning supplies. He takes what he needs from the court and avails himself of the enemy's grain, so his provisions suffice. Long transport lines to supply the troops impoverish a kingdom, and the farmers as well. At the same time, wherever the troops travel, prices go up. And once there is inflation, the farmers find their resources depleted. Then, the farmers will be hard-pressed to render service in the outlying areas. Ground down, with resources gone, the heartland will be emptied of viable households. Seventy percent of the commoners' ready cash will be used up, and nearly as much—some sixty percent—of the wealth of the ruling house lost, in the form of broken carriages and worn-out nags, money for armor, helmets, arrows and crossbows, for halberds and shields, spears and mantlets, bullocks and great carts.

The wise commander strives to feed his army with the enemy's provisions. For every cartload of grain seized from the enemy he saves twenty on his own side, and for every bushel of fodder from the enemy, twenty are saved from his own stores. Therefore, although killing the enemy is all a question of rage, wresting advantage from the enemy is something else, a question only of wealth. Therefore, in chariot battles, you should reward the person who first captures ten or more chariots, and switch out the flags and banners. Those chariots can then be added to your own. Treat the captured infantry well. This we call "victory over the enemy, even as you increase troop strength."

In arms, those who value victory eschew lengthy engagements. The commander who understands his troops is a virtual god mandating the fates of his subordinates. Likewise, he is the chief agent who either makes the ruling house safe or imperils it.

CHAPTER 3

PLANNING
AN ATTACK

謀攻

are inferior, then give ground. But if your troops are much inferior, you'd best evade the enemy. "A smaller force's stubbornness in sticking to a plan makes it easy prey for the larger force."[6]

Now, as we all know, the good field commander is the chief support of the realm. If the support is sturdy on all four sides, then the realm will be strong. But if the support is flawed, the realm will always be unstable. Therefore, there are several ways the ruler may imperil his armies:

If he fails to understand when the army cannot advance or retreat, and he orders them to do so. (This is a classic case of hobbling the troops.)
If he fails to understand the respective tasks of his Three Armies,[7] and he governs them all in the same way, then his army officers will be confused.
And if he fails to see how to balance and synchronize the operations of his Three Armies, then his officers will doubt his competence.

Once the Three Armies are not only confused but also suspicious, then trouble from the local lords will surely ensue.[8] (This is a classic case of "inducing chaos in the army and throwing victory away.")

To realize victory, go by five paths: (1) by figuring out whether it is possible to fight or not; (2) by recognizing how many troops are needed for the task;[9] (3) by unifying the aims and ambitions of the high- and low-ranking; (4) by being prepared for the unexpected; and (5) by the ruler's refusal to meddle with his able commanders.[10] These five— they are the Way to taste victory.

And so I say, "Know the enemy; know yourself, and you will meet with no danger in a hundred battles. If you do not know the enemy, but you know yourself, then you will win and lose by turns. If you know neither the enemy nor yourself, you will lose every battle, certainly."

CHAPTER 4

FORMS TO PERCEIVE

Master Sun says,

Of old, those who excelled in battle thought first to make themselves invincible, and so they waited for the moment when their enemies could be defeated. It is you who determine your own invincibility, but whether the enemy can be conquered or not rests with him. Therefore, whoever excels in battle can make himself invincible, but he cannot always make the enemy *vulnerable*. Hence I say, "The conditions for victory can be known, but they cannot be forced."[1]

Go on the defensive when your enemy cannot be overcome.
Go on the offensive against a vulnerable enemy.
Defend when your troop strength is lacking.
Attack when you have surplus strength.

To excel at defense means hiding oneself away in the deepest recesses of the earth.

To excel at offense means striking from the high-
est reaches of the heavens.

Therefore, the commander who is good at both
offense and defense can preserve himself and
achieve total victory.

A victory that does not surpass the understanding
of the vulgar crowd is not the best sort of victory.[2]
Nor is the finest way to win a battle one that the
whole realm applauds.

Just as

> Lifting the tip of an autumn hair doesn't mean
> you're strong.
> Seeing the sun and moon doesn't mean you've
> got keen eyes.
> Hearing a thunderclap doesn't mean your ears
> work well.

In antiquity, those who were deemed good generals achieved victory over the easily defeated.

Therefore, he who excels in battle doesn't have a
name for cleverness, nor does he garner accolades

for his courage. He never errs in winning battles, because he places his men where they are bound to win, and he conquers those who are already lost. [[So those who excel at battle take a stand where they cannot be defeated and never squander the chance to defeat the enemy.]]† Thus the troops who win care most about victory, and less about doing battle, and the troops liable to defeat care most about going into battle and less about seeking victory. The commander good at deploying troops cultivates these ways and holds to these rules.[3] Therefore, he can make policies that lead to victory or defeat.

The art of war consists of:
1. measurements;
2. estimates;[4]
3. calculations;
4. weighing;
5. victory.

The terrain leads to measurements;
The measurements lead to estimates;
The estimates lead to calculations;

† Double brackets indicate a possibly interpolated text.

The calculations lead to weighing the options;
The weighing leads to victory.[5]

Thus victorious troops come down as heavily as
a ton against an ounce, and the reverse is true
for the defeated army. The victors, in sending
their men into battle, may as well be opening the
floodgates into the steepest ravine.[6] So the form
becomes clear.[7]

CHAPTER 5

THE DISPOSITION OF POWER

勢

MASTER SUN SAYS,

In general, ordering the multitudes is just like ordering the few, in that it requires a division into units. Battling the multitudes is just like battling a few, in that it requires a distribution of duties and titles.[1] The multitudes who comprise the Three Armies can be made invincible, when under attack. It is simply a matter of calculating the odds for a surprise versus a conventional engagement.[2] When troops are added, they should come down hard, like a whetstone hurled at eggs. It is simply a matter of "empty" versus "full."[3]

In general, conventional methods engage the enemy, while surprise secures victory. Thus, by definition, to be good at unleashing surprises is

to be as various as the cosmos itself,
to flow as inexhaustibly as the Yellow and
    Yangzi Rivers,

to begin afresh as constantly as the sun and
moon,
to turn like the seasons, bringing new life, even
from death.

There are no more than Five Notes, yet the variations on them can never all be heard. There are no
more than Five Colors, but the variations on them
can never all be seen. There are no more than Five
Flavors, but the variations on them can never all
be tasted. There are but two battle strategies, the
conventional and the surprise, but, used in combi-
nation, they produce an infinite number of variations. "Surprise" and "convention" engender one
another, like a bracelet or a ring, with no beginning or end. Who can exhaust their variations?

A surge of rapids can send boulders crashing,
because of the disposition of the land. A down
swoop by a bird of prey can destroy the victim,
because of the timing. So it is with the commander who excels in battle. Finding his position dangerous, with a slim margin of error,[4] he
takes up a position that makes him murderous as
a drawn crossbow, and as swift in his timing as a
trigger-release.

Even amidst the tumult and clamor of battle, he remains unperturbed. Despite the churn and blur, with an enemy bearing down on him with a force like that of primeval *qi*, he may appear to be encircled and nonetheless be unbeatable. Disorder is born from order; cowardice, from courage; weakness, from strength. Wresting order from disorder depends upon a proper division of the army units; wresting courage from cowardice depends upon assuming a strategic position; wresting strength from weakness depends upon making a certain show. Thus the commander who is expert at drawing out the enemy will first show his opponent something that he is sure to follow, dangling a piece of bait that he cannot resist. Using such ploys the commander gets the enemy to make his move, at which point the commander ambushes him.

So, the expert commander seeks victory from strategic position; he does not demand that his men deliver a victory. He is able to select the right men to exploit the advantages gained from strategic position. He sends those men into battle with the force of rolling logs and boulders. It is the nature of logs and boulders to lie still on flat ground, but put them on steep slopes and they come barreling down. [[Square objects tend to be stationary, but round objects tend to roll. So it is that the strategic position of the expert commander can be likened to rolling round boulders down a steep high mountain.]][5] This defines the strategic disposition of power.

CHAPTER 6

WEAK AND STRONG

虛實

Master Sun says,

In general, whoever takes his position first on the battleground to await the enemy can take his time, whereas the commander who takes up his position belatedly must rush into battle hard-pressed. By definition, those who excel in battle compel the enemy and they do not let others compel them. It is beneficial to the enemy if he can come of his own accord, and a hindrance if you prevent him from arriving on schedule.[1] Thus to manage to wear down a well-rested enemy, to starve a well-provisioned force, or to dislodge them from a safe perch—all these happen only when you have lured the enemy out of the place where he could feel unhurried, so that he must rush to a place he never intended to go.[2]

Only in unoccupied territory can you march a thousand leagues without growing weary. Only

with an undefended place can you attack, fully
confident that you will seize your objective. Only
when defending an unassailable place can you be
certain of holding your position. Thus, facing an
expert in offense, the enemy does not know where
to defend, and facing an expert in defense, the
enemy does not know where to strike.

So veiled and subtle is he,
His moves nearly invisible.
So marvelous, miraculous,
Virtually soundless, he strikes.
Like a god deciding the enemy's fate.

An advance too powerful to resist means burst-
    ing through the weak enemy lines.
A withdrawal that evades pursuit means speed
    too great for capture.

So if our country wants to fight, we see to it that
the enemy has no choice but to do battle with
us, even when he is behind high walls and deep
moats. We force him to engage with us in battle
by attacking what he must save. But if our country
has no desire to fight, we make it impossible for
the enemy to engage us, even if we have no better

protection than a line drawn in the sand. In either case, we have thrown him off course.

So long as we determine the enemy's forms while concealing ours, we can concentrate our forces while he divides his. If our army is united and the enemy's divided, that is using a force of ten to attack one; we are many to his few. Given that our country has legions of men to attack small forces, then those who would confront us in battle are bound to find their numbers reduced.

The place we have chosen to give battle must be kept secret. If the enemy cannot anticipate us, he will have to prepare to defend many positions, and then the enemy units doing battle with us will be fewer. Thus, if the enemy prepares to reinforce his front, his rear is weakened, and if he prepares to reinforce the rear, his front is weakened. And so it goes with the left and the right. To be prepared everywhere is to be strong nowhere.

A position is weak when one force makes preparations against another, and stronger when one forces others to prepare for *it*.

Those who can anticipate the place and day of the engagement can march a thousand leagues to join the battle. But for those who cannot anticipate the place or day of battle, their left flank

cannot rescue the right, nor their right the left;
their front cannot rescue the rear, nor their rear
the front. This is even more true when reinforcements get separated by a few leagues, let alone tens
of leagues. As I see it, even if the troops of Yue[3]
are many, what good is this to them in terms of
victory? Thus I say, Victory can be made! For even
though the enemy has strength in numbers, we
can prevent him from fighting us.

Therefore, calculate the probabilities, to better
understand the likely gains and losses. Provoke[4]
him [so that he makes his move], to better understand his characteristic patterns of motion and
stillness. Make the enemy assume visible form, to
better understand the ground for life and death.
Prod and jab him, to see which positions have surplus strength or too little.

The ultimate skill in determining formations
lies in assuming no set formation. If there is no
form, then their spies embedded in your camp
will not be able to discern it, nor will the wisest
of their counsellors be able to lay plans against it.
Cleaving to *their* form, you plant victory in their
midst, even before they know what has befallen
them. Others all learn the formulae that supposedly won me victory, yet no one can fathom the

process by which I won. And so I say that victories in battle cannot be repeated by would-be imitators; armies must assume their forms in response to infinitely changing circumstances.

The formation of the troops is like water. Just as water's flow avoids the high ground and rushes to the low, so, too, the victor avoids the enemy's strong points and strikes where he is weak. As water's flow follows the forms of the land, so, too, the winning army varies its tactics, adjusting to the enemy's formations.

Now, the army should not have a constant position or a permanent form. The capacity to respond to the enemy's changes, and so seize victory, we call "divine." Therefore, just as no one of the Five Planets[5] is always dominant, and none of the four seasons has a constant place, the sun has shorter and longer days, and the moon waxes and wanes.

CHAPTER 7

CONTENDING ARMIES

軍爭

MASTER SUN SAYS,

In general, the rule for mobilizing and deploying troops is this: the commander receives his orders from the ruler, at which point he assembles his armies by gathering multitudes, he forges them into a well-coordinated unit, and then he makes camp facing the enemy.[1] No task is more demanding than the contest between armies, whose difficulty lies in straightening a winding path, and turning trouble to one's own advantage. Make the enemy follow a circuitous route and lure him on with offers of benefits, and you will arrive before him, even if you set out later. This is a case of understanding how to use devious, rather than direct, tactics. So the contest between armies can bring profit or peril.

If you mobilize your entire force, thinking by this to secure some advantage, you will surely be too

late to reap it. On the other hand, if you aban-
don part of your army in hopes of securing some
advantage, you will surely lose your equipment
and supply wagons. For this reason, if the commander, scheming to win some advantage, has his
army pack up its armor and set off in haste, stop-
ping neither day nor night, force-marching at double time for a hundred leagues, then

> Commanders in the Three Armies will all be
>   taken hostage;
> The strong will be forced out in front;
> And the tired lag behind.[2]

So, by this method, only one-tenth of the army
will arrive on time.

But if the army travels only fifty leagues a day
to vie for an advantage, then you will likely lose
only one good commander, *and* by this method,
half your force will arrive on time. Traveling only
thirty leagues a day means fully two-thirds of the
force will arrive on time. By any reckoning, an
army lacking its supply wagons will perish, as will
an army lacking provisions or an army that fails to
commandeer supplies methodically along the way.

So, if you don't know the designs of the

local lords,[3] you cannot predict how best to engage them. And if you don't know the local topography—the mountains, forests, ravines, marshes, and wetlands—you won't know where to march your troops. Nor can you take full advantage of the local terrain, unless you use local guides.

Therefore, troops rely on deception to gain ground, moving only after the advantages have been calculated; their formations suddenly divide and rejoin units. By such means do the troops become swift like the wind, yet calm like trees in a forest. And by such means do they consume like a raging fire, while remaining as unmoved as a mountain. They become as hard to fathom as shadowy forms and as startling as thunderclaps. When plundering the countryside, divide your numbers. And when extending your territory, divide the spoils generously. Weigh the pros and cons before making any move. Whoever knows both the devious and direct tactics in advance will surely triumph. This is the rule for the contests between armies.

The *Army Regulations* states: Because commands cannot be heard in battle, use drums and gongs. Because units cannot readily identify one another in battle, use flags and pennants. Drums, gongs, flags, and pennants are the means to coordinate men's ears and eyes. Once the men are of one heart and mind, the brave will not be able to advance on their own initiatives nor the cowardly retreat. This is the best way to manage the masses of men.[4] Thus in night battles make extensive use of torches and drums, whereas in battles during the day, make extensive use of flags and pennants. These are the tools that can alter men's perceptions.

The Three Armies can be demoralized and their commanders made to lose heart. Now, in the morning, the enemy's morale is high. By noon, it begins to flag. By evening, the enemy feels drained. Thus, to command morale, the commander who is expert at deploying troops avoids the enemy when he is high-spirited, but he strikes when their energies are flagging. To command hearts and minds, he meets the enemy's disorder with good order, and his panic with utter calm. To command the utmost physical power, he confronts the enemy who has come from afar on a battlefield near him, pitting his own well-rested and well-fed troops against exhausted and starving enemy troops.

Do not intercept an enemy whose array of

banners is perfectly uniform. Do not attack an enemy whose flags are in perfect order and whose formations are disciplined. By such means, the commander can master the whole range of contingencies. Therefore, the rules of deploying troops are these:

Do not attack an enemy who has the high ground.
Do not go against an enemy that has his back to a hill.
Do not follow an enemy that feigns retreat.
Do not attack the enemy's crack troops.
Do not take the enemy's bait.
Do not stop an army on its way home.
When surrounding the enemy, leave him a way out.
Do not press an enemy who feels cornered.

These are the rules for deploying troops.

CHAPTER 8

NINE CONTINGENCIES

九變

MASTER SUN SAYS,
In general, the rule for deploying troops is this:

Once the commander receives his charge from the
    ruler, he assembles his armies, and gathers his
    multitudes.
He refuses to make camp in difficult terrain.[1]
He meets with others at the major thoroughfares.
He takes care not to tarry in terrain where he can
    be cut off.
He makes plans if the terrain is liable to encirclement.
He battles to the death, if the terrain offers no way
    out.[2]

There are
roads he will not travel,
armies he will not strike,
walled cities he will not attack,
terrain he will not contest.

Nor will he accept and obey each and every one of the ruler's commands.

Thus a commander with a thorough grasp of the advantages to be had from the Nine Contingencies will surely know how to deploy his troops, while the commander who fails to grasp these essentials will not be able to wrest any advantages from the terrain, even if he knows the lay of the land. Failing to appreciate the arts of managing the Nine Contingencies, anyone who would command the troops will likewise not be able to secure the most from his men, even if he understands the five methods to take advantage of the terrain.[3]

For this reason, the wise commander never misconstrues or fails to ruminate on the advantages and disadvantages.[4] As he takes advantages into account, his hard work pays off in reliable ways. Taking disadvantages into account, he finds a way to extricate himself from trouble. Thus to subjugate the local lords, he uses the threat of harm; to keep them in his service, he gives them tasks to do; and to lure them on, he dangles the prospect of gain.

So, the rule for deploying troops is this:

Do not count on the enemy not coming.
Depend instead on your side being prepared to
    confront him.
Do not count on the enemy not attacking.
Depend instead on your side having an unassail-
    able position.

So a commander may have five fatal flaws:

One determined to fight to the death can be killed;
One determined to survive at all costs can be
    captured;
One with a quick temper can be provoked by
    insults;
One obsessed can be sullied and disgraced;
One who would spare the people grief can be
    overburdened.[5]

In general, these five dangers in a commander can
prove fatal when he is deploying troops. One or
more of these five traits is invariably the cause for
an army's rout and the slaughter of its commanders. A good commander must give the most careful consideration to these five.

CHAPTER 9

FIELDING THE ARMY

行軍

MASTER SUN SAYS,
In general, to position the army and size up the enemy, these rules apply:

In crossing mountains, keep to the valleys and face the open ground.[1]
Keep to the high ground;[2] and
In the heat of battle, do not scale the mountains.[3]
This is the right way to field an army in the mountains.

In crossing perilous waters, distance yourself from the water as soon as possible.
When the invader is in perilous water and coming your way, do not meet him in the water.
If you let half of their force cross[4] before you attack, that is to your advantage.
Those eager for the fray should not meet the invaders near the water.

Take a position up high facing open ground,
    and do not go near the water's flow.
This is the right way to position an army near water.

In crossing perilous salt marshes, the key thing is
    to rush through and brook no delay.
But if you must engage the enemy in the midst
    of salt marshes, stick to the water grasses [that
    allow your troops firm footing], and place your
    back against the stands of trees.
This is the right way to position an army on salt
    marshes.

On the flatlands, position yourself on level
    ground.
Put your army's stronger forces on the right, with
    the higher ground at their backs.
Make sure the battle stays in front, with the safe
    area behind.[5]
This is the right way to position an army on
    flatlands.

The Yellow Emperor defeated the Four Lords by
gaining an advantageous position for his army in
these four different situations.[6]

In general, an army prefers high ground and dis-
likes the low ground. It values sun and safety,
not the dark and danger. It aims to increase its
chances of survival by taking up a position on
solid ground with ample resources. And when
an army experiences none of the hundred mala-
dies to which it is prey, then it will certainly win.
With rises, hills, embankments, and dikes, it positions itself on the sunny side, with the right flank
turned with its back to them. This is good for
the troops, because it exploits the terrain to best
advantage.

When it is raining upstream, so the waters
come gushing down, wait for them to settle, before
crossing.

With steep river gorges, natural wells, box can-
yons, dense cover, quagmires, natural traps, and
crevasses, beat a quick retreat and certainly do
not approach. Keep a distance from all of these, and
you may force the enemy to draw near them. Face
these and the enemy will have to put them behind
him. If the army on the march meets[7] steep
ravines, pooled marshlands, reeds and rushes,
mountain forests,[8] and tangled undergrowth, you

must diligently scour them, as these are the very
places where ambushes are laid and spies hide out.

If the enemy is close but quiet,
He relies on his strategic position.
If the enemy, although far away, throws down
    the gauntlet,
He wants others to advance first.
When he positions himself on level ground,
    it is because he thinks it gives him the
    advantage.
If whole stands of trees move,
Troops are coming.
If there are blinds and barriers in the grasses,
Suspect the worst.
If birds take to flight,
He is sure to be lying in ambush.
If animals stampede in fear,
He is mounting a surprise attack.
If the dust rises high in spirals and funnels,
His chariots are coming.
If dust blankets the ground,
His infantry are arriving.
If the dust disperses in patches,
His firewood details have been dispatched.[9]
If a few dust clouds come and go, here and there,

He is making camp.
If his rhetoric is modest, yet his army continues
    to improve its preparedness,
It means he will advance.
If he is belligerent and advancing aggressively,
It means he will withdraw.

If his light chariots come out first,
And take up positions on the flanks,
He is going into battle formation.
If he has suffered no setback, yet he sues for
    peace,[10]
He is plotting.
If he is rushing, and putting his troops in
    formation,
He's decided that "it's high time to start!"[11]
If some of his troops advance while some retreat,
He is seeking to lure us forward.

If the enemy soldiers lean on their weapons,
They are hungry.
If those sent for water take the first drink
    themselves,
They are thirsty.
If there is an advantage to be had yet they do
    not advance to seize it,

They are weary.

Wherever birds gather,

The enemy position is unoccupied.

When there are shouts in the night,

The enemy is frightened.

When there is turmoil within the ranks,

The commander is not respected.

When their flags and pennants are shifting
    about,

The enemy is in chaos.

When his officers are easily angered,

The enemy is exhausted.

When the enemy feeds his horses grain, and his
    men get meat,[12]

And when his men no longer hang up their
    water flagons, or return to camp,

The now-desperate enemy is ready to fight to
    the death.

Where, hemming and hawing, the enemy com-
    mander speaks to subordinates in a meek
    and halting voice,

He has lost his men.

When he metes out too many rewards,

He signals that the enemy is in trouble,

And when he metes out too many
   punishments,
He signals that he is in dire straits.
The commander who erupts violently at his
   subordinates, only then to fear them, is
   totally inept.
When the enemy's emissary comes with concil-
   iatory words,
That's a case of wanting to cease hostilities.
When an angry enemy confronts you for an
   extended time, without either joining you
   in battle or quitting his position, you must
   watch him with the utmost care.

In war, it is not numbers that give the advantage.
It suffices if you do not advance recklessly, are able
to consolidate your own strength, get a clear pic-
ture of the enemy's situation, and secure the full
support of your men. It is only the one who makes
no careful plans and takes his enemy lightly who
is certain to be captured by him. If you punish
troops who are not yet attached to you, they will
not obey, and if they disobey, they will prove hard
to manage. But once you have gained their devotion, if discipline is not enforced, you cannot use

them either. Therefore, command them with civility and keep them in line with strict military discipline.[13] This will ensure their allegiance.

If commands are consistently enforced in training the men, the men will obey. If commands are not enforced during training, the men will not obey. The consistent enforcement of commands benefits both the men and their commander.

~~~~~~

CONFORMATIONS OF THE LAND

地形

MASTER SUN SAYS,

The conformations of the land include:

1. open,
2. hanging,
3. split,
4. defiles,
5. ravines,
6. distances.

"Open" describes lands where both armies can reach one another. With them, whichever army first occupies the sunny high ground and establishes secure supply lines will have the advantage in battle.

"Hanging" describes lands where advance is possible, but return is hampered. With them, you will likely defeat only the enemy who is unprepared. With a well-prepared enemy, you can go out to meet him on such a battlefield, but you won't necessarily defeat him. Moreover, you'll be hard-pressed to beat a retreat, and so find yourself at a disadvantage.

"Split" describes lands that disadvantage whoever attempts the first incursion, on either side, yours or the enemy's. With them, you should never engage the enemy first. Even if the enemy tries to bait you, refuse to engage, for it's better to let the enemy come halfway out, and then attack, at which point you will have secured the advantage.

With defiles, occupy the land first, and await the enemy with the passage fully garrisoned. Should your enemy occupy the defile first, filling it with *his* men, never go after him. However, if he fails to fill the space within the pass, go after him.

With ravines, it's best to occupy them first, taking the high ground to await the enemy. Should your enemy occupy them first, it's best to pull out and retreat; do not go after him.

With distances, both sides enjoy equal advantages. It is not easy to provoke a fight, and engaging the enemy confers no advantage.

These six constitute the arts of the terrain. Given that they are the commander's ultimate responsibility, he must investigate them thoroughly.

In warfare, there is desertion, insubordination,
peril, collapse, chaos, and rout.
These six are hardly due to natural catastrophes;
they are the commander's fault.

Desertion follows one army attacking another ten
   times its size, when the strategic advantages are
   equal on both sides.
Insubordination follows when the infantry is
   eager to fight, but the officers are weak.
Peril follows when officers are eager to fight, but the
   foot soldiers are weak.
Collapse comes when unbridled rage consumes a
   senior officer, so much so that he moves without authorization to engage the enemy and fails
   to understand his capacities.
Chaos comes when a weak commander fails to
   enforce the regulations *and* delivers instructions that are far from clear, so that his officers
   and men cannot be trusted and his military formations are in disarray.
Rout comes when a commander proves incapable
   of assessing the enemy, so he sends a small force
   out to engage a large, a weak force to attack the
   strong, or he operates without crack troops as
   backup.

These are the six routes to certain defeat. Given that they are the commander's ultimate responsibility, he must investigate them thoroughly.

Thus the conformation of the land can aid the troops in battle. The best commander assesses the enemy's position and creates the conditions for victory. He analyzes hazards and calculates distances. Applying his understanding of such factors to the battle at hand, he is certain to win, but should he disregard them, he is certain to lose.

Thus if the way he goes into battle guarantees victory, the commander-in-charge must insist on fighting, even if the ruler forbids the engagement. And if the way he is directed to go into battle will not allow a victory, he must refuse to fight, even if the ruler insists that he do so.

We call the "ruler's treasure" the commander who advances without any thought of winning personal fame for himself, and who withdraws despite the prospect of punishment, as his sole concern is to protect his men and promote his ruler's interests.[1] Because he looks after his foot soldiers tenderly, as if they were beloved sons, they follow him into the deepest ravines, and even die willingly by his side.

But

If he indulges them, and can't make them do his
bidding,

If he spares them and can't command them,

Or if he is too erratic to govern them, they will be
spoiled children, good-for-nothing.

What will halve your chances of victory is this:

To know your troops can attack but not understand the enemy is not open to attack.

To know the enemy is vulnerable, but not understand your own troops cannot attack.

To know the enemy is vulnerable and your troops
can attack, but still fail to understand whether
the terrain favors battle.

Thus he who knows arms is never misled when he
makes his move. He is never at a loss when he ini-
tiates an action. Whence the saying:

Know the enemy and your own,
And victory is in sight.
Know the terrain and timing,[2]
And victories will be total.

CHAPTER 11

NINE KINDS OF GROUND

九地

MASTER SUN SAYS,
In the art of deploying troops, the key contingencies on the ground are

Deserters' ground,
Land taken lightly,[1]
Land worth fighting for,
Meeting ground,
Ground serving as a crossroad,
Land never taken lightly,
Land difficult to cross,
Land made for an ambush,
Deadlands.

Whenever a powerful local lord in his own
domain goes himself into the field, it is "deserters'
ground."

Whenever the incursion into the enemy territory is not deep, it is "land taken lightly."

Contested ground whose occupation confers an advantage to either side, theirs or ours, is "land worth fighting for."

Ground equally accessible to both sides is a "meeting ground."

Where the borders of several neighboring domains converge and the first to arrive has the potential to secure a crowd of supporters is, by definition, a "crossroad."

Deep incursions into enemy territory that leave, at your back, many of the enemy's walled cities and towns: that's land that is "never taken lightly."

Mountains and forests, passes and defiles, and wetlands—any ground that is hard work to cover—that we call "difficult to cross."

Entrances and exits so narrow or winding that even small enemy forces can attack our legions— that's "land made for an ambush."

Terrain where you survive only if you battle ferociously we call "deadlands."

This being the case, never fight on deserters' ground.

Never tarry when on ground taken lightly.

Never attack the enemy on ground worth fighting for.
Never get cut off on meeting ground.
Always seek to make allies on crossroad lands.
Always pillage on lands not taken lightly.
Always press on in difficult grounds.
Always be ready with strategies in lands made for an ambush.
And always, always in the deadlands, fight like hell.

The commanders of old acclaimed for their expertise in deploying troops were able to force the outcomes, whereby

the enemy's vanguard and rear guard could not reach each other;
the enemy's main unit and its auxiliaries could not support each other;
the enemy's officers and men could not save one another;
the enemy's superiors and subordinates could not maintain communication lines;
the enemy's foot soldiers, once separated, could not regroup;

the enemy troops, once assembled, could not form
   ranks.

When these expert commanders deemed it
advantageous, they moved into action. Otherwise, they never budged. Suppose someone posed
the question, "How should we prepare for an
enemy fortified with great numbers and with
strict discipline, who is about to advance on us?,"
I would reply, "If you seize whatever he values
most, before he can prevent you from doing so,
you will have his ear."

A most important consideration in war is speed.
With speed, you can exploit whatever is beyond
the enemy's reach; you can take the routes he
least expects, and you can attack him before he's
prepared.

In general, the guidelines for the "guest" army
invading are these:

The deeper the penetration into enemy territory,
   the greater the invader's cohesion, so the host
   army may not prevail.

Plunder the enemy's most fertile fields, and your entire army will have plenty to eat.

Pay special attention to your troops' food rations and do not tire them out.

Lift their morale and build up their strength.

Employ stratagems that make your troop movements impossible to predict.

Throw your troops into situations where they have no way out, and they will confront death and never retreat. Once the troops are fighting to the death in the knowledge that they have, in fact, no alternative, your officers and men will give their all.

When your troops are most trapped,
They will not panic.
Faced with no retreat,
They will stand fast.
Though deep into enemy territory,
They stay tight.
With no options,
They enter the fray.
Thus the troops stand ready, with no need of prompting,
Without demands, they succeed.

With no sworn oaths, they feel close as kin.
Even with no orders, they can be trusted.
Forbid good omens, get rid of the rumors,
And going to their deaths, they will not waver.

If our soldiers do not have surplus wealth, it is not because they despise worldly goods. And yes, they may not live long, but not because they despise the thought of longevity. On the day these officers and their men learn that they have been called to do battle—whether they have been sitting around in camp or lounging on the ground—each man will react to the news by sobbing until tears soak his cheeks and collar. But throw them into a situation with no way out and each man will display the monumental courage of a Zhuan Zhu or a Cao Mo.[2]

Therefore, the real experts at deploying troops are like the "sudden striker" snake at Mount Heng. If you strike its head, its tail snaps round; if you strike its tail, its head snaps round; and if you strike its midparts, both head and tail snap round. If you wonder whether the troops can be trained to act as virtual "sudden strikers," I would reply to you, "They can. The men of Wu and Yue loathe each other, but if they happened to be crossing a river in the same boat and were caught by gale

winds, they would surely rescue one another, as
naturally as the right hand helps the left."

To prevent soldiers from scattering, it has
never been enough to count on tying up horses
and burying chariot wheels. The *only* way to manage the troops consists of making them equally
resolute, so that they act as one. And success in
exploiting all manner of terrain comes down to
knowing the configurations of the land.[3] By such
means, the real expert guides his legions as easily
as if he were leading a person by the hand. They
see no alternative but to follow.

In performing his duties, the field commander
remains calm but unfathomable, disciplined and
self-governed. He puts blinders on his officers
and men, so they never know what he's thinking.[4]
He alters his plans and strategies, so that no one
is cognizant of them. He changes his camp, and
takes roundabout routes, so that others cannot
divine his movements. Sallying forth to the des-
ignated spot, with his men in train, he acts like
a man who kicks away the ladder once he has
climbed to a great height. Leading them deep
into enemy territory, he pulls the crossbow's trig-
ger. He burns his boats and breaks his cooking
pots. He drives them hither and thither, like a

shepherd herding his sheep, and no one knows where they are headed. He masses the forces of his entire state, and then he plunges them into danger. Such are the urgent affairs of the field commander.

The measures needed to cope with the nine types of ground, the advantages to be gained by flexible maneuvering of the army, and the basic patterns of human character—these must all be thoroughly investigated.

For an invading army, the methods to use in general are these:

The deeper you penetrate into enemy territory, the more single-minded your troops will be.

The less deeply you penetrate, the more easily your troops will desert.

Once you leave your own domain and your army crosses the border into enemy territory, you have entered terrain where you can be cut off with no way to turn back.[5]

When you have access to all sides, you're at a crossroad.

When you have invaded deep into enemy territory, you're in land that is never lightly taken.

When you have penetrated only a short distance,
   you're in land easily taken.
When your back is to secured ground, and you
   face a narrow defile, you're in land made for an
   ambush.
And when you've nowhere to turn, you are in the
   deadlands.

Therefore, on land where the troops can easily desert, our commanders should make sure to unify
their wills. On ground easily taken, they should
make sure to keep the troops together. On contested ground, they should make sure to force the
rear to pick up the pace. At any meeting ground,
they should pay particular attention to defense. At
any ground that serves as crossroad or thorough-
fare, they should take the opportunity to solid-
ify our alliances. On land not easily taken, they
should ensure, at all cost, that the food supplies
continue. On land that is difficult to cross, they
should make sure to push ahead along the road.
On land liable to ambush, they should make sure
to block off any escape routes.[6] On deadland, they
must show the troops that survival depends upon
their willingness to die.[7]

Thus the inclination of the soldier is

Resist when surrounded,
Fight when you have to.
Follow orders when pressed to the verge.

Unless you know their intentions, you cannot
enter into alliances with the rulers of neighboring states in advance.
Unless you know the lay of the land—its mountains and forests, its passes and defiles, its
wetlands—you cannot deploy an army on it.
Unless you can employ local scouts, you cannot
take advantage of the terrain.
If an army fails to act wisely in even one of these
respects, it is not fit for a hegemonic leader.
Until you employ local guides, you cannot take
advantage of the terrain.
When an army of a hegemon attacks a large state,
it prevents the enemy from gathering its forces.
And when its awe-inspiring might bears down on
the enemy, it prevents the enemy from joining
forces with its allies.
In this way, a true leader neither jockeys for alliances with other states, nor cultivates his influence throughout the realm. Rather, by trusting

in his own plans, and bringing awe-inspiring might to bear down on his enemy, he easily plucks the walled cities of the enemy and topples its ruling house.

If you give out extravagant rewards and issue unexpected orders, you can compel the entire army as easily as one man. Compel them to do their duties, but never reveal your plans. Drive them with rewards, but never reveal the hardships. Only if you throw them into life-and-death situations will you survive. Only if you plunge them into places with no way out will you and your men stay alive. Now, as we all know, only when the rank and file are endangered will you wrest victory from defeat.

Therefore, the business of waging war lies in careful study of the enemy's designs. "Focus your strength in a single direction / And you can kill the other commander a thousand leagues away." This we call "realizing your objective by wits and skill." So, on the day war is declared, close off the passes, tear up any agreements, forbid any further contact with enemy emissaries. Rehearse your plans thoroughly in the palace and the ancestral temple, so that you may execute your plans. When the enemy gives you an opening, rush in. Tempt him with whatever he lusts for, and then by subtle means determine the date for battle. Never let him know the timing of your attack. The only steadfast rule is to adapt to the enemy's moves, in order to determine the course and outcome of the battle. So,

> At first, move like a modest maiden,
> And the enemy will open his door.
> Later, be as swift as a hare on the run,
> And any resistance will prove too late.

CHAPTER 12

ATTACKS
WITH FIRE

火攻

MASTER SUN SAYS,
The five kinds of incendiary attacks are: (1) setting
fire to personnel; (2) setting fire to stockpiles of
supplies; (3) setting fire to the baggage trains and
supply wagons; (4) setting fire to the granaries and
armories; and (5) setting fire to everything along
the routes between encampments having possible
reinforcements.

When deploying fire, there must always be flam-
mable materials for it to consume, and those
materials must always be on hand. There are
appropriate times to light fires in an attack (when
the weather is dry and hot), and appropriate days
to raise fires (the days when the moon is located
in one of the four constellations, Winnower,
Wall, Wing, and Chariot Axle).[1] Typically, on
those days the winds pick up and carry the sparks
everywhere.

In general, you must adapt to whatever changing situations may arise with these five types
of attack. If you manage to set a fire inside the
enemy camp, you must go in as soon as possible,
but if the enemy's troops remain calm, despite
an outbreak of fire, bide your time and do not
attack. Let the fire reach its height, and if you
can follow through, do so. But if you cannot,
stay where you are. If you see the potential to get
an agent to set a fire from a location outside the
camp, don't wait until he infiltrates the camp. Set
the fire as soon as the time is right. If the fire is
set upwind,[2] don't attack downwind.[3] Know that
while the wind may blow throughout the day, it
tends to stop at night.

In general, the army must be made to fully understand the rapid turns of fortune that can come
from the five fire attacks, and you must protect
them by your calculations about timing.

> With fire's help, attack—and guide its course.*
> With water's help, attack—and wield its force.*
> Water can cut the foe off, true.*
> But will not seize his goods for you.*

Disaster, by definition, is failing to capitalize on your achievements despite victory in battle and seizure of the spoils.[4] As the phrase goes, "He who hesitates is lost." Hence the saying, "The brilliant ruler thinks it through, while good commanders refine the plan."

> When nought's to gain, move not.*
> Over things of little worth, fight not.*
> Save in direst need, war not.*

A ruler cannot call up armies in a rage nor can his commanders start a war over a slight. They move only if it is to their advantage. They bide their time, if it is not. A person in a rage can be restored to good humor, and someone mortally offended can be restored to affability. By contrast, a kingdom, once destroyed, cannot be restored, nor can the dead be brought back to life. Thus the brilliant ruler approaches battle with due prudence, and good commanders are ever on their guard. This is the way to secure the ruling house and keep the army intact.

CHAPTER 13

USING SPIES

用間[1]

MASTER SUN SAYS,

As a rule of thumb, raising 100,000 troops and
sending them out on campaign to a location
1,000 leagues away[2] costs 1,000 units of gold/
per day, including the expenses incurred by the
Hundred Families and the upkeep by the ruling
house. This creates upheaval in the palace and
beyond, in the inner provinces and at the fron-
tiers.[3] You can count on 700,000 taking to the
roads, idle and weary, since they are unable to
attend to their usual tasks. The armies on both
sides may be at a standoff for several years, with
decisive victory finally determined in a single
day. Yet there are those in power who begrudge
the few hundred gold ingots[4] needed to confer
ranks and emoluments on spies, and so they act
in complete ignorance of the enemy situation. To
begrudge the expense is the height of inhuman-

ity. Such a person is neither a good commander for his men nor a good aide to his ruler. He is no master of victory.

Thus, it is their foresight that allows the perceptive ruler and the wise general to mobilize and conquer others, achieving merit far beyond the vulgar crowd. Such foresight does not come from the spirit world. One cannot discern the inherent pattern based solely on past events, or prove it by measuring the stars.[5] It must come from other people—those with the requisite knowledge of the enemy's situation. Accordingly, five kinds of spies are to be employed: locals, insiders, double agents, "dead" spies, and live agents. When all five kinds are set in motion, and no one knows their operations, they form a "net devised by the gods" of immense value to the ruler.

> Locals are the enemy's compatriots in our
> employ.
> Insiders are enemy officials in our employ.
> Double agents are enemy spies who report to
> our side as well.

"Dead" spies are pawns in our employ whom
we intentionally deceive, so that they relay
false information to the enemy.[6]
Live agents, by contrast, report back to us.

Therefore, nothing is closer to the Three Armies
than their spies,[7] and none deserves greater reward
than the spy. Yet no affairs should be more secret
than those relating to spies.

Only the most perceptive ruler understands how
to employ spies, and only the most humane and
just commander knows how to put them in the
field. Only the most subtle interrogator can get the
whole truth out of spies. What delicacy and finesse
are required! Yet no one can possibly succeed without using spies. Where a case of espionage has been
divulged prematurely, not only the spy but every-
one he confided in must die.

As a general rule, it is always necessary to know
ahead of time the family and personal names of
the defending commander, his retainers, counsellors, gate officers, and sentries, whether it's an
army we want to attack, a city to be besieged,

or an assassination to carry out. We must direct
our spies to find a way to secure this information for us. It is equally necessary to discover
whom the enemy has sent to spy on us. They can
then be employed as double agents, so long as we
offer them bribes and win them over[8] before giv-
ing them their instructions and releasing them.
Availing ourselves of these double agents, we can
recruit and employ locals and insiders. By the
same token, we can learn what false information
to feed the "dead" spies, so that they inform the
enemy of it. Relying on their familiarity with the
situation, our live spies can complete their assign-
ments on schedule. To recapitulate: the ruler
must have full knowledge of the covert operations undertaken by these five kinds of spies. And
since the double agent is key to all intelligence-
gathering, the ruler must be made to see that
he is the operative to be treated with particular
generosity.

Of old, the rise of the Yin ruling house was due
to Yi Yin, who once served the house of Xia; likewise, the rise of the Zhou house was due to Taigong Wang, who had served the house of Yin.[9]
Thus only the most perceptive and wise generals—

those who can get the most intelligent men to be their spies—can fulfill their destinies and accomplish great things. In war, intelligence is of the essence, for it is what the armies depend upon in their every move.

GLOSSARY

bian 變: noun = contingencies; verb = to vary; also variables, turns of events; see also *quan*

bing 兵: arms, war, troops

ce 策: calculating, counting, tallying up (slips)

dao 道: way of governing

fa 法: regulations, models, institutions

guo 國: capital and court and, by extension, the ruling house and realm

jiang 將: field commander

li 利 . . . *hai* 害: benefit . . . harm . . .

qi 氣: energy, life-breath, in some cases what we would call adrenaline

qu 趨: hasten

quan 權: (literally, "weighing"); often this refers to the ability to adapt to changing circumstances

san jun 三軍: Three Armies (in Chunqiu)

shan zhan 善戰: those who excel in battle

she 舍: make camp

shi 勢: disposition, location, strategic position

shi 時: timing

shizu 士卒: This common phrase generally refers to those under a general's command. However, in one instance in Chapter 1, the text distinguishes between *bing* 兵 and *shizu* 士卒: "which army... which fighters?" (兵眾孰強，士卒孰練). The *Liji* also notes ritual obligations for the *shizu* 士卒, stating that when a noble (公) dies, "the *shizu* mourn and then return" (士卒哭而歸). According-ing to the *Shangjun shu*, the *shizu* were rewarded with land. Perhaps this suggests that *shizu*, at least in some instances, denotes a status that was above that of the lowest-ranking fighters in the army.

shou 守: defend

tian 天: weather, heavens, Heaven

tong 通: to have a thorough grasp

wei 微: nascent, hidden, subtle

wo 我: our [side] (usually referring to a larger community)

wu 吾: I ("We" in the "royal We")

wu 伍: defined by Cao Cao as five to ninety-nine soldiers

wu li 五利: Five Benefits or Advantages, acquired by those who understand "successful use"

wuxing 五行: Five Planets in their courses

xing 形: formation of the army; possibly position; *xing bing* 形兵: troop formation

zheng 政: administration of the realm, and policy making

zhong 眾: multitudes, masses

zu 旅: battalion—Cao Cao: 500 troops; *Guanzi*: 2,000 troops; *Zhou li*: 500 troops

zu 卒: century—Cao Cao: 100–499 troops; *Guanzi*: 200 troops; *Zhou li*: 100 troops

NOTES

INTRODUCTION

1. Sun Tzu (with or without a hyphen) is the transliteration of "Master Sun" in an older form of romanization called Wade-Giles, which was employed in the first translations by an English Sinologist (Lionel Giles, in 1910) and by an American (Samuel B. Griffith, in 1963). Since 1972, use of Wade-Giles has gradually declined in favor of the romanization adopted in the People's Republic of China (PRC) called *pinyin*, which renders "Master Sun" as Sunzi. Norton signals the older transliteration simply because it is more familiar to nonspecialists.

2. The scholarly literature debates the date for the start of Zhanguo, aka the Warring States.

3. *The Art of War,* Chapter 13. Compare Chapter 2, which gives equally off-putting figures for the cost of war.

4. Simon Goldhill reportedly made this observation in a lecture, with regard to the competitive study of Greek. From the early empires down to today, game boards akin to those of Monopoly sets have plotted the ups and downs of careers at court.

5. "The Supreme Art of war is to subdue the enemy

without fighting.—Sun Tzu," Donald Trump tweet (July 17, 2012). I thank Richard Curt Kraus for this information.

6. For a Chinese critique of Bannon as an interpreter of ancient texts, see Ed Zhang, "Bannon Misreads Sun Tzu in Going to Economic War," *Global Times* (August 21, 2017).

7. Bob Dreyfus, "Sebastian Gorka, the West Wing's Phony Foreign-Policy Guru," *Rolling Stone* (August 10, 2017).

8. David Lauterborn, "Secretary of Defense James Mattis," *Military History Magazine* (December 1, 2016), www.historynet.com/interview-with-general-james -mattis.htm (accessed August 28, 2018).

9. *The Art of War,* Chapter 11, returns to this theme: "The *only* way to manage the troops consists of making them equally resolute, so that they act as one."

10. William Davies, "Everything Is War and Nothing Is True," *New York Times* (February 23, 2019).

11. *The Art of War,* Chapter 13, seems to contradict this on first reading, as it says, "Such foresight does not come from the spirit world. One cannot discern the inherent pattern based solely on past events, or prove it by measuring the stars. It must come from other people—those with the requisite knowledge." What *The Art of War* acknowledges is that history never repeats itself, so current knowledge must reflect new developments and new ideas. However, insight into human behavior is always relevant, if not decisive, in judging any unfolding situation, as other chapters in *The Art of War* remark.

12.   Nor is there any reason to see either China or the United States as exceptional, contra the overly simplistic views of Henry Kissinger, who discusses Sunzi's *Art of War* in a recent book chapter called "The Singularity of China." See Kissinger, *On China* (New York: Penguin Books, 2012), 59–60.

13.   See https://www.nytimes.com/2019/01/24/us/politics/nancy-pelosi-donald-trump.html.

14.   Chris Hedges's 2002 classic, *War Is a Force That Gives Us Meaning*, had him writing, "In the beginning *war* looks and feels like love. . . . It can give us purpose, *meaning*, a reason for living. Only when we are in the midst of conflict does the shallowness and vapidness of much of our lives become apparent." Martin Jay's recent interview with the *American Herald Tribune* (January 17, 2019), like his *Refractions of Violence,* argues cogently (contra Stephen Pinker's ahistorical analysis) that modern society is increasingly violent.

15.   Su Shi (1037–1101), writing "On Guan Zhong" (Guan Zhong lun 管仲論).

16.   Alfie Kohn, "Science Confirms It: People Are Not Pets," *New York Times* (October 27, 2018), confirms that scientific research on the efficacy of rewards shows that we can't bribe others into doing what we want.

17.   *The Art of War*, Chapter 1. However, Chapter 13 insists that the spirit world does not confer foresight.

18.   As *The Art of War,* Chapter 9, says, "It suffices . . . to . . . secure the full support of your men." The able commander gains his troops' devotion, but he also disciplines them, as needed.

19. Chapter 6: "Victory can be made! For even though the enemy has strength in numbers, we can prevent him from fighting us."

20. See *The Art of War,* Chapter 10, for this exhortation and talk of its reward: "victory is in sight."

21. *The Art of War*, Chapter 10.

22. *The Art of War*, Chapter 1.

23. *The Art of War*, Chapter 4. I say "his and her" here, because over the years historians of China have found more and more evidence about impressive female commanders. This theme will be explored in the forthcoming Norton Critical Edition of *The Art of War*.

24. *The Art of War*, Chapter 8. Compare Chapter 11, which talks of the commander realizing his objective "by wits and skill."

25. *The Art of War*, Chapter 4.

26. *The Art of War*, Chapter 8.

27. *The Art of War*, Chapter 11.

28. *The Art of War*, Chapter 11.

29. For the propensities of the modern nation-state, one may consult Carl Schmitt, as summarized in Hans Sluga, *The Politics and the Search for the Common Good* (Cambridge: Cambridge University Press, 2014), esp. pp. 133ff.

30. The principal members of the Berkeley working translation group are: Nicholas Constantino, Benjamin Daniels, Andrew Hardy, Joseph Passman, Frederick Tibbetts, Trenton Wilson, and Zheng Yifan. Other experts in the United States and abroad were consulted during the translation process. I thank them all for their contributions. I owe particular thanks to

Benjamin Daniels and Trenton Wilson for helping me consider how to craft this introduction.

A Note on the Text

1. Ji Tianbao's precise dates are unknown. Most scholars, such as Li Ling, date him to the Northern Song without supplying further details. Gawlikowski and Loewe give the dates 11th–12th century; see "Sun tzu ping fa," in *Early Chinese Texts*, ed. Michael Loewe (Berkeley: University of California Press, 1993), 450. Loewe notes that a defective edition of Ji Tianbao's text with eleven commentaries is dated to 1195–1224. Xie Xianghao 謝祥皓 dates him to the last two emperors of the Northern Song, Zhezong and Huizong (1085–1127); see Xie's *Sunzi zhi* 孫子志 (Shandong renmin chubanshe, 2009), 222. The Ji Tianbao version originally had only ten commentaries, but an eleventh was added in the Southern Song period, so there are two versions (a ten- or eleven-commentary version) today.

2. An *Art of War* manuscript excavated from a tomb at Yinqueshan 銀雀山 in 1972 (probably between 140 and 118 BCE), incorporating the thirteen chapters found in the received text, contains many variants, some of which change the meaning of the text. Moreover, the Yinqueshan manuscript contains several extra chapters, showing that ancient compilers tended to add (or subtract) units of text as they saw fit. This extra material has been ably translated by Roger Ames in his *Sun-Tzu: The Art of Warfare* (New York: Ballantine, 1993).

CHAPTER 1
FIRST CALCULATIONS 始計

1. *Guo* 國 (often translated as "state") in early times refers to the court and capital, and therefore the ruling house (called *guojia* 國家). Sunzi (Wade-Giles romanization, Sun Tzu) literally means "Master Sun," an honorary title, where Sun is the family name. "Sacrifice and war" are identified as the two great affairs of state in *Zuozhuan*, Zuozhuan, Duke Cheng, Year 13 (國之大事, 在祀與戎).

2. Several commentators take this as, "If you heed my assessments, when you dispatch troops into battle, this means certain victory, and I will stay. However, if you do not heed them, dispatching troops would mean certain defeat, and so I intend to leave." However, this translation does not quite explain the construction using a verb + *zhi* ("it"). Ames and Mair follow Chen Hao 陳澔 (1261–1341), who takes *jiang* to mean "I am about to do it," rather than the noun "field commander." This comes close to language found in Liu Xiang's discussion of "remonstrance" in the *Shuoyuan* "Chen shu" 臣術 chapter.

3. Or, "that in itself creates a favorable strategic disposition . . ."

4. "Beyond" can mean at least four things here, so we have left the translation purposely vague: (1) Cao Cao identifies *wai* 外 as "beyond conventional models or rules" (*changfa zhi wai* 常法之外), i.e., the unexpected. (2) Beyond the court = *wai*, as in the expression *wai jiao*. (3) Zheng Yifan, a member of the Berkeley

group, suggests that *wai* may refer to the troops already in the field. (4) "Beyond" may refer to whatever happens after the initial setup.

5. This overtranslates a single five-character sentence that conveys both these ideas.

6. Each bamboo or ivory tally or strip (*suan* 筭) corresponds to one calculation or set of calculations made in the planning phase of the military campaign. These calculations are eventually rehearsed in the temple so that the overall plan for battle can be finalized in the presence of the ancestors. Those holding more tallies or strips have done more "homework" and so they are better able to assess and adapt their plans to the enemy, so they will likely win. As in our culture, the gods help those who help themselves (as Algernon Sydney and Benjamin Franklin agreed).

CHAPTER 2
INITIATING BATTLE 作戰

1. Glues and lacquers refer, in the most literal sense, to the joining together of products, from war chariots to the handles of axes. At the same time, in the metaphorical sense, they can refer to the greasing of palms (rewarding people, etc.) to secure the services of allies and subordinates or the more subtle "social glue" binding members of a community together.

2. Ames here has *qi yong zhan, gui sheng* (values victory), from Yinqueshan.

3. Suffice to make up the losses.

CHAPTER 3
PLANNING AN ATTACK 謀攻

1. Usually from 100 to 200.

2. This has a more economic flavor than "alliances" (or "allies") carries.

3. Usually the translators have taken these lines as fully parallel: attacking/disrupting their plans, attacking/disrupting their alliances, attacking/disrupting their soldiers, and attacking/disrupting their walled cities. Cao Cao seems to say that if the enemy has a set plan, it can be attacked.

4. *Zuozhuan* always uses *quan* 全, a principle of wholeness, intactness.

5. Here we follow several earlier translators (Li Ling, Guo Huaruo, and Victor Mair), who argue that the phrase should read *bei ze fen zhi* (倍則分之, meaning "if double, then divide them"), not *di ze feng zhi* (敵則分之, meaning "if it's the enemy, then divide them"). Ames is one of several commentators to oppose this emendation, not because of the Yinqueshan parallel (as none exists for this section), but because of Wu Jiulong's commentary.

6. Tentative translation. Many commentators take this more or less as Ames, p. 112, does: "Thus what serves as secure defense against a small army will only be captured by a large one." Some commentators, however, read *jian* as "firmness," i.e., stubbornness in sticking to a plan, despite the particularities of the situation; hence this translation. Earlier we read the two sentences as parallels: "[In such a way,] a smaller force can remain strong, and a greater one be captured."

7. The largest domains boasted of having Three Armies, with multiple divisions.

8. Two obvious sorts of trouble that might ensue are aggression from neighboring rulers and a weakening of alliances.

9. Conceivably this line could also mean, "recognizing how to deploy larger and smaller troops" in the field.

10. Even the Eastern Han "Confucian" text entitled the *Bohu tong* concurs, arguing that a ruler should temporarily refrain from treating a field commander as a subject when he is commanding his troops, because "those inside the capital cannot be governed by those outside the court, and soldiers cannot be governed by those inside the court. One wishes to develop (the field commander's) authority and make his the only commands" 國不可從外治, 兵不可從內御, 欲成其威, 一其令.

Chapter 4
Forms to Perceive 形

1. Put another way, "Victory can be foreseen but it cannot always be achieved."

2. Alternately, "To appear victorious in a way that everybody can appreciate is not the best win."

3. For *zheng* 政 (policies), the Yinqueshan counterpart writes the homonym *zheng* 正 (to align or be an arbiter of).

4. This could also mean "provisions."

5. The thinking behind the translation is this: the terrain determines the size [of the contested territory];

the size of that in turn determines the calculations [regarding the probable quantities of resources needed to wage a successful war]; the calculations determine the number [of troops to be deployed]; that number in turn determines the balance of power; and the balance determines who is victorious.

6. This might be called "piling it on."

7. The line is somewhat cryptic. It may be that the victors are so relentless due to their formations, or that this is the form that the able commander visualizes.

CHAPTER 5
THE DISPOSITION OF POWER 勢

1. We follow the suggestion of Herrlee G. Creel, the famous Sinologist (1905–1994), regarding the phrase *xingming* 形名 (in *What Is Taoism? and Other Studies in Cultural History* [Chicago: University of Chicago Press, 1970]) while noting that Cao Cao, basing himself on the *Mozi*, talks instead of "pennants and drums" or "pennants and unit markings." Mo Di, putative author of the *Mozi* (Master Mo), supposedly lived c. 470–c. 391 BCE. Mozi (aka Mo tzu, Mo Di), who hoped to stop offensive wars, was famous for organizing his followers in military bands that excelled in defensive warfare. He would then send them wherever they were needed, to relieve sieges and unprovoked attacks.

2. The commentaries do not agree on how to define these antonyms.

3. "Empty" and "full" each has more than one sense:

(1) unprepared vs. prepared; and (2) empty spaces vs. packed; (3) to strike the enemy's vulnerable points ("empty") while evading his strengths.

4. Alternatively, for *jie duan* 節短: "his timing is rapid."

5. I suspect this material in double brackets is an interpolation, a commentary that has crept into the main text.

CHAPTER 6
WEAK AND STRONG 虛實

1. The language here recalls the language used in sacrifice of inviting the gods to the ritual, to have them come down to dwell among men. Two alternative translations are also plausible: (1) "The ability to make the enemy come of his own accord depends upon your offering him benefits; the ability to prevent the enemy from arriving at a given place depends on your harming him." (2) "It will be beneficial to make the enemy ..."

2. The Yinqueshan counterpart to this passage writes *chu qi suo bi qu* 出其所必趨 (to leave the place where he will always be hurried), as the Cao Cao commentary seems to. The *Shijia ben* simply says *bu qu* 不趨 (unhurried), which requires a change in subject: "Whoever is good at battle leaves his place in no great haste" (said of the good general, not the enemy). One Song edition reads *bu yi* 不意 (not intentionally, by surprise).

3. The troops of Yue would be far away, in all likelihood, to Sunzi's readers.

4. Li Ling's version reads *hou* 候 ("to watch") instead of "to provoke."

5. This use of *wuxing* 五行 has always been taken to refer to the Five Phases, but that category is a later construction, according to the latest scholarship. Probably this refers to the Five Planets in their courses, as argued in Marc Winter, "Suggestions for a Reinterpretation of the Concept of *wuxing* in the *Sunzi bingfa*," *Bulletin of the Museum of Far Eastern Antiquities* 76 (2004), 129–62, esp. 138; cf. Nylan, "Yin-yang, Five Phases, and *qi*," in *China's Early Empires: Supplement to the Cambridge History of China*, vol. 1, ed. Michael Nylan and Michael Loewe (Cambridge: Cambridge University Press, 2010), 369–97.

CHAPTER 7
CONTENDING ARMIES 軍爭

1. Li Quan 李筌 simply reads "makes camp," but Li's reading seems to be something of an outlier. The "Ten Questions" 十問 manuscript from Yinqueshan (vol. 2, pp. 193–94) begins each question in its list with the phrase *jiao he er she* 交和而舍, as here. The context there makes it clear, as do most of the commentaries, that the meaning of this phrase is "to set up camp facing the enemy," reading *he* 和 as the name of the camp gate.
2. These lines do not rhyme.
3. As it is not clear whether the nobles are enemies or allies, the translation here remains neutral.
4. The Cao Cao commentary glosses the lines in this way.

CHAPTER 8
NINE CONTINGENCIES 九變

1. Presumably, "lands where he and his army can be cornered."

2. These Nine Contingencies lay out the unforeseen turns of fate that may occur, for which possibilities the good commander plans.

3. We cannot be sure what the "five methods" are. Cao Cao says these are the *wu shi* 五事, a term with multiple meanings: Five Usages; Five Forms of Mastery; Five Sharp/Critical/Key Tools; Five Instrumental Calculations. Perhaps "Five Sharp Moves" comes closest.

4. Reading *za* 雜 as the verb "to mix up"; however, one gloss defines *za* as "to exclude from one's deliberations," with the implication that the commander then misunderstands the situation. The translation tries to capture the full range of possibilities that this single verb implies.

5. Alternatively, "he can be overencumbered"; "he can be given additional troubles."

CHAPTER 9
FIELDING THE ARMY 行軍

1. Some think *shi sheng* is "facing the sun," but this reading cannot be maintained throughout the chapter. Below, the *sheng* refers to "safe ground." The Yinqueshan counterpart is differently transcribed here.

2. Cao Cao says that *sheng* refers to the sunny side.

3. The text supplies no object for the verb, but English virtually requires it. We imagine troops trying to scale mountains, for this is the topic here.

4. Trenton Wilson, a member of the Berkeley Translation Group, based on Chapter 10 ("it's better to let the enemy come halfway out"), prefers "Let them get halfway across the river." This is a reasonable reading as well.

5. The rationale here seems to be this: because the enemy then has to cross the dangerous ground to get to your main forces.

6. Presumably, Shaohao, Zhuanxu, Taihang, and Yandi. One might compare the text "Huangdi Fights the Red Emperor" 黃帝伐赤帝 in the Yinqueshan version, which some take to be an extra Sunzi chapter.

7. Yinqueshan says *jun pang* 軍旁, "to the side or flank of the army."

8. *Shanlin* 林木 ("forests") appears in some editions, but *shanmu* in Yinqueshan (as here).

9. Tentative translation. Yinqueshan has no counterpart to this. We follow Li Quan the commentator here, as do Giles and Ames.

10. Equally possible are two other renderings: "If out of the blue, they sue for peace . . ." or "If, without making prior stipulations, the enemy sues for peace."

11. Meaning, first, that the enemy is eager to enter the fray; and, second, that he may be pushing up the date for battle.

12. The Southern Song edition (compiled between 1127 and 1194) of the text, with Cao Cao commentary, entitled *Wei Wudi zhu Sunzi* 魏武帝註孫子 has a variant: 殺馬肉食者, 軍無糧也 (meaning, "When

they kill their horses for meat, / The troops are out of supplies").

13. The commentaries say that this means gaining their allegiance by humane treatment. On the *wen/wu* distinction, see the chapter by Nylan and Yin in the forthcoming *Norton Critical Edition* of this volume.

CHAPTER 10
CONFORMATIONS OF THE LAND 地形

1. Or, perhaps, "align his interests with those of his ruler."
2. Literally, "the heavens," which can also refer to local climate.

CHAPTER 11
NINE KINDS OF GROUND 九地

1. I.e., without incurring a great cost.
2. These are famous assassins, with Cao Mo the more famous of the two, judging from the extant texts at our disposal.
3. The commentaries speak here of "hard and soft," which can refer to the quality of the land or to lands "difficult or easy to cross."
4. *Analects* 8/9 says of the Way that you can make people perform it, even if you cannot make them understand it. However, it would be unwise to push the parallel too far, since *Analects* 13/30 also says that it is immoral to take "uninstructed" troops into battle.

5. This term is new, and not one of the nine mentioned earlier. Note, too, that even where the same terms are used, they are not cited in the list in the same order as above.

6. This may refer to access and retreat, or to the psychological dimension; this means "to unify their will," as Cao Cao says.

7. This could also mean "show our [commander's] resolve to fight to the death with them."

ATTACKS WITH FIRE 火攻

1. Wall marks the fall equinox and Winnower, the winter solstice. Axle and Wing correspond to either side of the spring equinox.

2. I.e., against the direction the wind is blowing.

3. Or possibly, in a downdraft.

4. As the Cao Cao commentary puts it, the spoils should be used to bribe and whip others into acting on your behalf.

USING SPIES 用間

1. The Chinese term is literally "those who 'get between' the parties."

2. Roughly 350 miles.

3. The Chinese simply says "inner and outer," which can

refer to domestic vs. foreign affairs, but also "inside the palace and outside." The annotations of Wu Renjie in the Sanlian Shijia edition take this to mean, "front lines and the rear troops."

4. Presumably these are commoners who are not soldiers. The phrase "on spies" is not in the Chinese original, and conceivably the line could refer to commoners who must pay to feed and shelter soldiers on the march.

5. This line is a bit obscure, but certainly it's talking about making calculations based on the regular movements of the stars and planets.

6. One way to regard them is spies who have been compromised by design, so Ames calls them "expendable" spies. However, their key attribute is that they are planted within the enemy camp to deliver, in all innocence, false information (by analogy to deadwood?), so even if they are tortured, they cannot supply real information. Of course, if their information is found to be useless or worse than useless, they may eventually be executed, but that is true of all five kinds of spies.

7. There is a possible wordplay here.

8. "Win them over" is one possible translation here, but *dao* as a verb or noun often refers to the mission. Hence the possible overtranslation of the line.

9. Yinqueshan mentions Su Qin here, which is anachronistic; in addition, most considered Su Qin morally suspect, whereas Yi Yin and Taigong were moral exemplars.